Ostriches

by Grace Hansen

Abdo
SUPER SPECIES
Kids

abdopublishing.com

Published by Abdo Kids, a division of ABDO, PO Box 398166, Minneapolis, Minnesota 55439.

Copyright © 2017 by Abdo Consulting Group, Inc. International copyrights reserved in all countries. No part of this book may be reproduced in any form without written permission from the publisher.

Printed in the United States of America, North Mankato, Minnesota.

052016

092016

THIS BOOK CONTAINS
RECYCLED MATERIALS

Photo Credits: iStock, Shutterstock

Production Contributors: Teddy Borth, Jennie Forsberg, Grace Hansen

Design Contributors: Laura Mitchell, Dorothy Toth

Cataloging-in-Publication Data

Names: Hansen, Grace, author.

Title: Ostriches / by Grace Hansen.

Description: Minneapolis, MN : Abdo Kids, [2017] | Series: Super species |
    Includes bibliographical references and index.

Identifiers: LCCN 2015959214 | ISBN 9781680805475 (lib. bdg.) |
    ISBN 9781680806038 (ebook) | ISBN 9781680806595 (Read-to-me ebook)

Subjects: LCSH: Ostriches--Juvenile literature.

Classification: DDC 598.5--dc23

LC record available at http://lccn.loc.gov/2015959214

Table of Contents

Big Birds! 4

Body 10

Eggs & Chicks. 18

More Facts 22

Glossary 23

Index 24

Abdo Kids Code. 24

Big Birds!

Ostriches are the largest bird **species**. The next largest bird is the emu.

emu   ostrich

Ostriches can grow up to 9 feet (2.7 m) tall. That is taller than a professional basketball player.

9 ft

6 ft 8 in

7

Ostriches can weigh 200 to 300 pounds (91 to 136 kg). That is about the same as a panda bear!

Body

Ostriches have long necks.

They have two large eyes.

Ostriches have the largest

eyes of any land animal.

Ostriches have long, strong legs. They use their legs to run fast. They can run up to 40 miles per hour (64 km/h)!

Each ostrich foot has two toes. The front toes have long, sharp claws. Ostriches use them to fight **predators**.

14

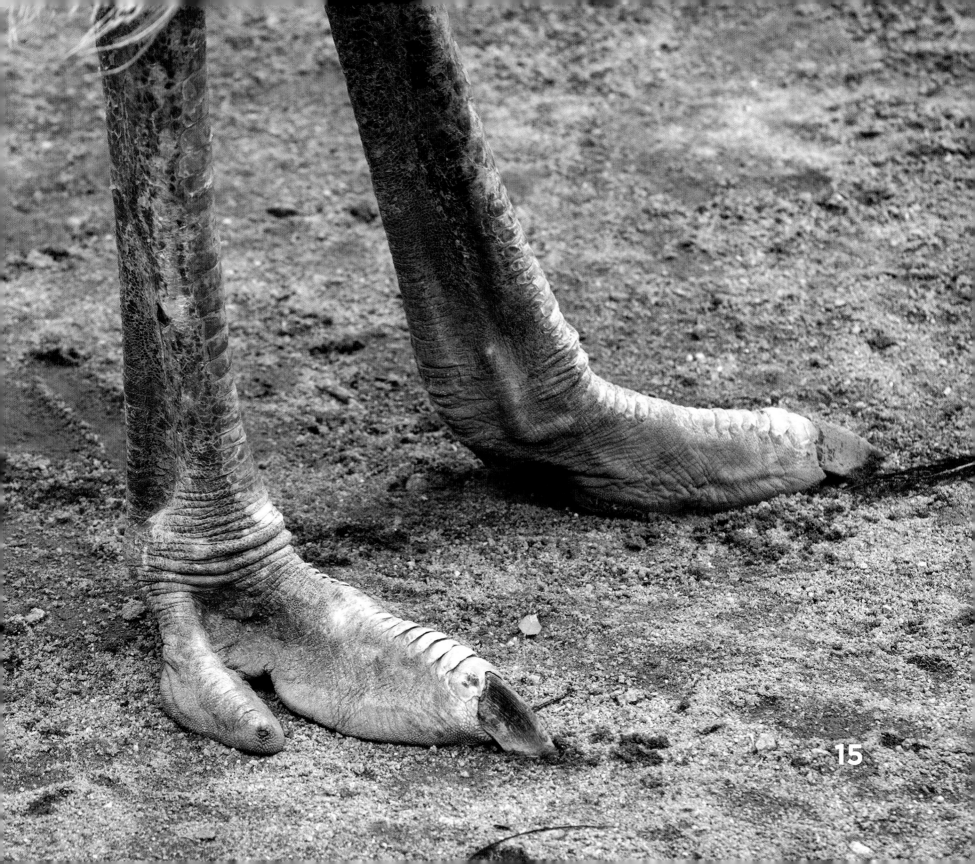

Ostriches cannot fly. Their wings are too short. Their wings have a use though. Wings help an ostrich **balance** and turn as it runs.

Eggs & Chicks

Ostriches lay huge eggs!

One ostrich egg weighs

the same as 24 chicken eggs.

Ostrich **chicks** are also big.

A newly hatched chick is the

same size as an adult chicken.

At six months old, they will be

their parents' size.

chicken

ostrich

21

More Facts

- Ostriches have lots of soft feathers. Males have black and white feathers. Females have brownish feathers.

- Ostrich **chicks** can run nearly 30 miles per hour (48 km/h) at 30 days old!

- Ostriches can cover a lot of ground while running. One step can be 10 to 16 feet (3 to 4.9 m) long!

Glossary

balance – to move without losing control or falling.

chick – a baby bird.

predator – an animal that lives by hunting and eating other animals.

species – a group of animals that are similar and can produce young animals.

23

Index

chick 20

chicken 20

claws 14

egg 18

emu 4

eyes 10

foot 14

height 6

legs 12

neck 10

panda bear 8

predator 14

run 12, 16

size 4, 10, 18, 20

speed 12

toes 14

weight 8, 18

wings 16

abdokids.com

Use this code to log on to abdokids.com and access crafts, games, videos, and more!

Abdo Kids Code:
SOK5475

24